NOT
In *My* Classroom!

BY TERESA MITCHELL

NOT
In *My* Classroom!

BY TERESA MITCHELL

Orange Hat Publishing
www.orangehatpublishing.com - Waukesha, WI

NOT IN MY CLASSROOM!
BY TERESA MITCHELL

"Ms. Mitchell's classroom is an exquisitely and efficiently run ship. She has established effective classroom procedures which allow her to teach and hold meaningful discussions with her students; with little to no off task distractions."

– **Paula Boyd**, Assistant Principal, Milwaukee School of Languages

Just in time for summer school and fall planning comes the debut classroom management guide by Milwaukee educator, Teresa Mitchell. With a focus on organization, structure, and student responsibility, this original guide and interactive planner helps teachers to minimize disruption in the classroom and offers tips on everything from seating arrangements and assignment schedules to successfully improving parent involvement. From elementary school to high school, Teresa's methods have proven effective in all levels of education, and continue to garner praise from fellow educators.

"She knows how to individualize and customize her lessons to fit all students, has patience- even when dealing with difficult children- and is the 'commander in chief' of time management."

-**Ms. Wanda Davis,** Behavior Intervention Classroom Teacher (BIC), Eastern Hills HS

As a seasoned educator, Teresa enjoys the challenges that have surfaced in today's education system. Her desire to teach and create global citizens has driven her to create an instructional tool for teachers to help solve modern classroom challenges. In the future, Teresa looks forward to creating programs for students and teachers to help close the academic gap and change the current approach to public education.

NOT IN MY CLASSROOM! has been published by Orange Hat Publishing, and will be available for sale in digital and hard copy formats through Amazon and Barnes & Noble. For questions regarding sales or publicity, contact Shannon Ishizaki at:

Email: shannon@orangehatpublishing.com
Phone: 414-212-5477

Published by Orange Hat Publishing 2015

ISBN 978-1-937165-87-1

Printed in the United States of America

www.orangehatpublishing.com

IN ALL YOUR WAYS ACKNOWLEDGE HIM...
PROVERBS 3:6

I would like to thank God for giving me the knowledge, skills, experience, and people placed in my life to create this instructional tool. My grandmother Florece Henderson (who is my number one supporter), my Auntie Shirley (who is the reason I am an educator), parents (of course), teachers, family, friends, and students (yes, students) who have inspired me along the way during my educational process. My experience as a teacher has been astounding, and I am forever grateful for the continued love and support I receive.

Table of Contents

Introduction

This handbook is designed for both new and experienced teachers to create a productive learning environment. Teaching is a rewarding career, but often endures challenging circumstances when entering the world of children and adolescents. One must be able to not only capture the mind of an individual, but also hold that captivation throughout the school year.

If every teacher practiced strong classroom management skills, the student body would be more enriched, test scores would improve in low performing schools, and teachers would be able to keep students focused and engaged in their lessons.

In this handbook you will gain access to many tips and strategies on how to maintain a successful learning environment. Therefore, the entirety of this handbook should be read and practiced thoroughly before the first day of school.

What is Classroom Management?

Classroom management is the ability to structure and control your classroom in all aspects, including behavior, agenda, and the method with which you carry out your lessons. Sometimes, as teachers, we may have an unsuccessful lesson and need to re-teach, but we can eliminate a lot of re-teaching by having control of our classroom. Students often fail to grasp the concept of a lesson due to distractions from other students. Valuable class time is lost each day due to redirecting disruptive behavior throughout the school year, which is why it is important to exert authority in the beginning. *Authority Exertion* is enforcement of rules and expectations in your classroom. Remember, this is your domain and it should only be controlled by you.

Understanding the Needs of the Student

Students come from various backgrounds and lifestyles, which is why it's important to remember our own encounters with our teachers. The main need of a student is to understand that his/her teacher cares about their education and wants what is best for them. However, students need to understand that teachers are not here to be their friends, but to complete an important aspect of their education that will prepare them to be successful in life. Teachers need to teach life skills and ensure students are prepared for the future to become productive citizens.

Keep in mind that students come to school to have an academic need filled by YOU. In order to attend to the need, you must first understand it. Here's the secret to understanding any need of a student: know that students want positive attention in various ways. Do not focus all the positive attention on one student, but instead spread it throughout the classroom. In some cases it may be more challenging to seek, but it is important that it is sought.

In cases where there is a disruptive student, pull that student aside before or after class and tell that student what you need from him/her, and hold the child accountable for their actions. It is important that students are responsible for their actions, which is a life skill that should be embedded to decrease irresponsible behaviors. A lot of times when there is a disruptive student it is due to the fact that their need is not being met. He or she may have the need to be a leader, be assigned a specific duty, or have someone who is counting on him/her to perform a task. We may never know, but it is up to the teacher to determine the needs of each student.

Note: *Refrain from raising your voice or showing any tone of agitation. If that happens, it will only feed the disorderly atmosphere.*

It is natural to have preconceived thoughts about an individual based on his or her appearance, and sometimes that judgment is false. Prejudging the student will limit your ability to build a positive, fulfilling relationship that allows the student to thrive.

I remember having a student my first day of teaching who entered my class with his oversized pants hanging down. I immediately assumed he would be a troublemaker, but in reality he had a focused mind and wanted to make something out of his life. Do not judge based on appearance- that is the number one mistake of a teacher. We are here to mold them into better versions of themselves.

Teachers cannot make prejudice assumptions based on a student's appearance, because it will alter our thought process and reflect in our interaction with the student. Each student should be regarded in the same way, yet excel in individual ways.

Classroom Structure

When entering your classroom for the first time it is important to become acquainted with your room and feel comfortable with your surroundings. Teachers need to feel comfortable in their classrooms and own their domain by walking around and becoming familiar with the structure of the room.

Position your desk in an area where the students are visible to you, and you are visible to them. Students should not feel at any given time that their teacher cannot see or hear them. This brings us to the setup of the students' desks. Students' desks should be arranged in a fashion where the teacher can see any student from all angles of the classroom. No student should partake in the "hide me" technique (gravitating towards a spot in the classroom where they feel they are less noticeable).

I arranged the desks in my classroom into two semi-circles (an inner circle, an outer circle, and one desk in the center for me to sit during discussion). This helped me to see each student from any angle of the classroom, and denied the students the ability to hide. If possible, one semi-circle works best.

Note: *You should be able to see each student from the center spot when engaging in discussion.*

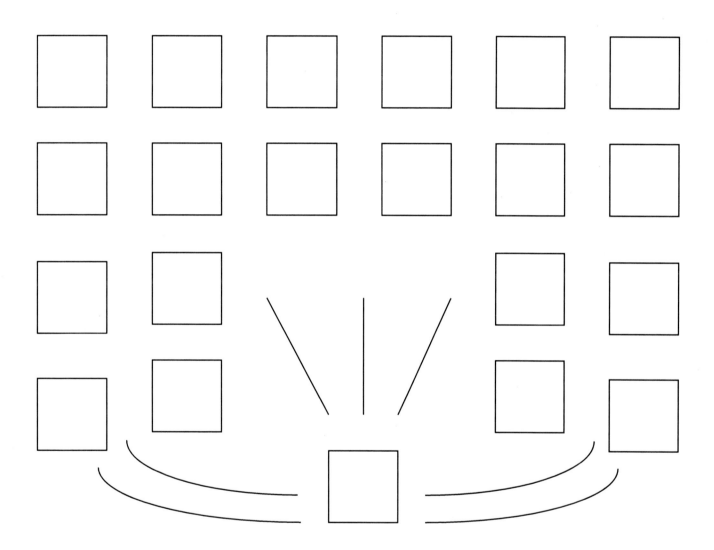

Begin brainstorming ways on how your class will be designed. You should not wait until the last minute to try and figure out the layout of your classroom.

_____ Classroom
Teacher's Name

Once the desks are arranged to your convenience, take a moment to walk around the classroom and between the desks. Make sure you have enough room to maneuver and keep students on task. Walking around the classroom is the number one way to keep students focused because they feel they are being watched.

Practice walking around the classroom with your eyes closed to become familiar with the setup. Therefore, you can focus less on where you are walking, and more on the actions of the students and lesson being taught.

This arrangement of desks also makes it easier to collect and hand things out. Students should take a sheet and pass the rest around, and vice versa for collecting assignments.

Seating Chart

A seating chart should be implemented at the beginning of the year and changed each marking period. By changing a student's seating they are adapting to different surroundings and peers, which is a life skill they will need in the working world. This also helps with learning students' names at the beginning of the year, and decreases behavioral problems throughout the school year.

Decorations

Your classroom should also be appealing to the eye. Content-focused posters should be displayed throughout the classroom. It is beneficial to have inspirational, content-specific quotes displayed around the top perimeter of your classroom. This prevents students from getting lost in their thoughts. Instead, their eyes can be attracted to a relevant quote. These quotes should get the students back on track to the lesson. Be creative!

Note: You never want a student's mind to become idle anytime during the class period.

Rules

Place your rules in four visible locations of your classroom. This makes students aware of expectations at all times, no matter where they are in the room. Instead of labeling your expectations as "Rules," try labeling it in a more positive manner, such as "Good Students Will." This gives the students the opportunity to display positive behavior, rather than feel as if they are being forced (especially with high school students). In some cases, students will rebel against rules and regulations because of their experiences, and we want to give them a chance to exert desired behavior.

Example:

```
┌──────────────────────────────────────┐
│ ┌────────────────────────────────┐   │
│ │         GOOD STUDENTS WILL:     │   │
│ │                                 │   │
│ │  • Not get out of their seat    │   │
│ │  without permission             │   │
│ │                                 │   │
│ │  • Not bring electronic devices │   │
│ │  to class                       │   │
│ │                                 │   │
│ │  • Bring necessary materials    │   │
│ │  to class                       │   │
│ │                                 │   │
│ │  • Participate in class         │   │
│ │  discussions                    │   │
│ └────────────────────────────────┘   │
└──────────────────────────────────────┘
```

Remember, your classroom is your domain, and you have full control of your classroom. Do not let any student overpower your authority.

What will your "Rules" list include? Choose an adjective to describe the type of student behavior you want to be practiced.

_____ STUDENTS **WILL:**

The First Day of School

The first day of school is the most important. You must first make sure to wear subtle colors (avoid bright, "friendly" colors). You want to give the impression that you are a teacher who means business. This is when you will capture the students by setting your rules and expectations. It is vital that they know you are a teacher who will not tolerate any distractions to the learning atmosphere throughout the school year. Be firm!

Agenda (Ready, Set, Go!): *Ready, Set, Go* is an agenda for students to know what to expect during the class period. Having an agenda will eliminate the question, "What are we doing today?" The agenda should include how much time students have to work on a specific activity. This instills a sense of urgency, and reduces the urge to socialize and procrastinate (a timer is a great tool to use).

Example:

Date:_____

Ready
Define Term (2 minutes)
Discussion (3 minutes)

Set
Build Background (5 minutes)
Activity (10 minutes)
Partner Sharing (5 minutes)
Discussion (5 minutes)
Reading (5 minutes)
Questions/Discussion (5 minutes)

Go!
Question (3 minutes)

Ready: What the students will begin the moment they enter your classroom. This should be on the board in a clear and concise manner. *Ready* should tell the students exactly what to do without the need for you to reiterate. The learning process begins the moment a student walks into your classroom and does not end until the time they leave. *Ready* is designed to get the students prepared for the lesson. For instance, if the students are going to be introduced to a new topic, have students define a relevant term to set the base of the lesson.

Set: The foundation of the lesson where you are teaching and engaging students. This may consist of various activities.

Go: Conclusion of the lesson where students answer a question in regards to what they have learned. This is a good way to reflect on the lesson to grasp an idea on how well the students understood the concept that was taught.

Example:

```
                               Go!
          Name_____  Date_____

      Answer to question: _____
      _____
      _____
      _____
```

Ready, Set, Go instructions reduce disruptions, because students are constantly working and trying to complete their tasks without being left behind. Students should have a sense of urgency, which should be established the first week of school.

I would inform my students that they had to complete the exit slip in order to receive credit for their assignments each day at the end of the class period. This took place in the last 2-3 minutes of the class to prevent students from packing up early or standing by the door. Also, it keeps them on track during instruction because they will be aware that they must complete the exiting assignment. The students should be exhausted at the end of the class period, not the teacher.

What will your agenda entail? Create your agenda for the first five days of school. It is a wise decision to have the first week of school thoroughly planned out because it will set the tone for the upcoming weeks. Students will already be frenzied, so you need to have a game plan for the first week to keep you calm.

_____ Agenda

Teacher's Name

NOTES

Course Syllabus

Students must receive a course syllabus that is to be sent home and signed by a parent on the first day of school. The course syllabus should include the following:

- ☐ Course Title
- ☐ Teacher's Name
- ☐ Teacher's Contact Information

Course Description

Give a brief summary of the course and how it will benefit the student. Parents and students want to know how this course will help them; what is the purpose? If a student (especially high school level) does not see the relevance in a subject, they may not take it seriously.

Objective

Students need a specific purpose for the course that will reappear throughout the school year. This is your main goal.

Class Expectations

Set high expectations for your students. Do not lower your standards and place students on a low expectation level. By doing this they will strive for the highest degree, which will make your job less challenging in the future.

Homework Folder

My students were given a homework folder to help keep track of assignments. Parents were to sign off each day there was an assignment to indicate awareness of homework on a regular basis. At the end of the week students received a weekly grade to keep parents informed of their child's progress. With this, parents and students are aware of their current grades and can improve (if needed) before grades are due.

Home Work Calendar (teacher's name and course)
Parents please sign each day of homework to indicate assignment completion.

Monday	Tuesday	Wednesday	Thursday	Friday	
Parent Signature _____ Oct. 3	Parent Signature _____ Oct. 4	Parent Signature _____ Oct. 5	Parent Signature _____ Oct. 6	Parent Signature _____ Oct. 7	Weekly Grade _____ Parent Initials _____
Parent Signature _____ Oct. 10	Parent Signature _____ Oct. 11	Parent Signature _____ Oct. 12	Parent Signature _____ Oct. 13	Parent Signature _____ Oct. 14	Weekly Grade _____ Parent Initials _____
Parent Signature _____ Oct. 17	Parent Signature _____ Oct. 18	Parent Signature _____ Oct. 19	Parent Signature _____ Oct. 20	Parent Signature _____ Oct. 21	Weekly Grade _____ Parent Initials _____
Parent Signature _____ Oct. 24	Parent Signature _____ Oct. 25	Parent Signature _____ Oct. 26	Parent Signature _____ Oct. 27	Parent Signature _____ Oct. 28	Weekly Grade _____ Parent Initials _____
Parent Signature _____ Oct. 31	Parent Signature _____ Nov. 1	Parent Signature _____ Nov. 2	Parent Signature _____ Nov. 3	Parent Signature _____ Nov. 4	Weekly Grade _____ Parent Initials _____

Behavior Log

Students were also given a behavior log that was placed in the folder. If there were any problems I would document the conflict in the behavior log and request a parent signature.

Behavior Log
Parents should sign off to indicate that they are aware of the issue.

Date	Behavior	Parents Initials

By creating a homework folder and behavior log, students feel accountable for their assignments and behavior. Although it may seem elementary for high school students, it works and teaches responsibility. Sometimes we have to go back to the basics to instill an effective work ethic in students.

Supplies

Inform students of materials needed to excel in your class. Supplying limited materials is sometimes necessary to teach responsibility.

Rules

Set your rules not only in the classroom, but in the course syllabus as well. Leave a message to your students that will reiterate your expectations. Also, include a sign-off page for every student and parent that requests a contact number and address.

It is important to be detailed in your syllabus to eliminate any future confusion.

Outline your course syllabus:

Teacher's Name_____

Course Title_____

Teacher's Contact Information_____

Course Description

_____

_____

_____

_____

_____

_____

Objective

_____

_____

_____

_____

_____

_____

Class Expectations

_____

_____

_____

_____

_____

_____

Supplies

-
-
-
-

Rules

Closing Statement

_____

_____

_____

_____

_____

_____

Down to Business:

At the end of the first day, students should receive a homework assignment that is due the next day. If you decide to use a homework calendar and behavior log, make sure students write down their assignment and get a parent's signature.

With some of my classes, I would not accept the assignment unless the parent signed off on it. Sometimes it takes a negative action, such as not accepting the assignment (no credit) to create positive practices among our students. Make sure this is included in the course syllabus if you decide to do so.

Assignments

An assignment should be given the first day of school to get the students back into the swing of things and ready for the remainder of the school year. We need to make our job easier by being organized and structured. It is a good idea to grade Monday- Thursday, and input grades each day. Therefore, when grades are due, you are not in a frenzy trying to meet the deadline. The more organized you are, the easier your job will become. Practice returning assignments back to the students the next day. It is important that you grade on a regular basis so you will have time to reflect and know if you need to re-teach a specific topic.

Your students should be aware of their progress on a regular basis so there are no surprises towards the end of the marking period. If you decide to use the "semi-circle" arrangement of desks, you can simply have students pass their homework folders to the left or right, and input their weekly grade while they are working on their independent assignment. You can also inform students that they will not receive their weekly grade unless the previous grade has a parent's initials (more responsible teaching).

Note: *Whenever you assign homework or class work, make sure the students receive their grade during the next class session. Therefore, you will need to grade on a regular basis. By doing this, the students can see the immediate pay off of their work. Whether it is positive or negative, they are able to properly associate the work they put forth with the grade they are receiving. Waiting too long to distribute grades can distant the students from their work, and reduce the impact the grade has on their conscience. Also, if you ever question a parent's signature or initials, contact the parent to verify.*

Activities

The following are examples of potential activities for the first day of school (secondary English).

One activity I partake in is "How it Feels to be Colored Me" by Zora Neale Hurston. We will read the excerpt and analyze the contents of the brown paper bag at the end of the story. This activity transitions into the homework assignment where students bring in items the next day that describes them. You can demonstrate what they are supposed to do by giving a brief presentation.

Another activity is to have students read, "We Wear the Mask" by Paul Laurence Dunbar. After explaining the significance of the poem, students can create their own masks using symbols describing themselves.

Both activities are a great introduction to symbolism. With the mask activity, when students are finished decorating their masks with symbols and colors, allow them to post them anywhere in the classroom. By doing this, students are gaining a sense of identity within the classroom. You want your students to feel comfortable and acclimated to their surroundings, and one way to encourage that is to continuously provide ownership opportunities.

When I allowed my students to place their masks wherever they chose, I was able to identify various students. For example, I noticed my students who enjoyed working with others placed their masks near other classmates. The students who were leaders did not mind placing their masks in isolation. It is also a good way to bring life to your classroom.

Relationship Building Assignment Creation

Assignment_____

Objective_____

Explain student exercise

_____

_____

_____

_____

_____

_____

Homework

_____

_____

_____

_____

How will this assignment benefit students?

_____

_____

_____

_____

_____

_____

_____

Relationship Building Assignment Creation

Assignment_____

Objective_____

Explain student exercise

_____

_____

_____

_____

_____

_____

Homework

_____

_____

_____

_____

How will this assignment benefit students?

_____

_____

_____

_____

_____

_____

_____

Relationship Building Assignment Creation

Assignment_____

Objective_____

Explain student exercise

_____

_____

_____

_____

_____

_____

Homework

_____

_____

_____

_____

How will this assignment benefit students?

_____

_____

_____

_____

_____

_____

_____

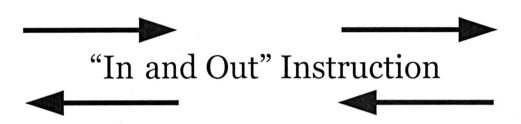

"In and Out" Instruction

In and Out instruction is when instruction begins the moment the student is "in" the classroom, and does not end until they are walking "out." Students must be occupied at all times while they are under your authority- there is no time for relaxation. Students must become accustomed to your teaching structure and know when they enter your classroom that it is non-stop until the bell rings to leave. It is not a bad thing when a student is lacking the energy to come to your class. This lets you know they are aware they have to participate under your instruction, and are prepared to work because it is expected of them. When a student reviews the agenda at the beginning of class they can prepare themselves for the daily tasks with no confusion.

In and Out instruction eliminates behavioral problems because the students are constantly working and know they must complete all activities during that class period, keeping in mind that they must complete their "Go" slip. Always set high expectations for your students and hold them accountable for their actions. A lot of times it is easy for a teacher to not hold a student accountable. However, when we loosen the reigns on accountability, we lose power. You never want a student to feel they are gaining power over you. Not only will they know it, but the other students will too.

During *In and Out* instruction you may have to slow the pace or get off track with the agenda if there is any confusion. If this happens, just mark it in your notebook, and pick up with it the next day. Rushing the lesson may cause you to miss something. Using a notebook on a regular basis is a good source to keep track of the lesson for each class.

Remember to constantly pace yourself- it isn't a race. I would rather go slow and have the students gain the concept, than fast and risk them missing what is important.

At the beginning of the class period when students are working on "Ready," you can take attendance quickly and pick up homework. When you are collecting the homework assignments, go to each student and allow them to hand the work to you. That way if a student chooses not to complete his or her assignment they will feel uneasy when it is their turn to hand it to you. If you come across a student who chose not to complete the assignment, you can take that opportunity to have a short, one on one conversation about what is expected of them. The goal is not to embarrass the student, but to make them feel accountable for their lack of effort. If it is multiple students, you can express your expectations and further stress the rules of your classroom to the students as a whole. As mentioned before, sometimes we need a negative action or feeling to get the desired outcome. You will only have to do this a few times before students catch on. Most students will not like the pressure of feeling that their progress is being noted in front of the class. However, when their progress begins to improve, be sure to acknowledge the positive effort and result in an equally public way.

If you choose not to pick up the assignments individually, have a homework basket at the classroom entrance for students to place their work. While you are grading the assignments you can write down names of those who failed to complete the work, and bring it to their attention the next class day. When bringing it to the attention of the students you can simply say "(Student name), I noticed you did not complete your assignment. Is there a particular reason why?" Whichever method you choose, students need to know you are not only aware, but that you also expect improvement.

NOTES

The Notebook

The notebook is your number one tool as a teacher when it comes to recollection of events. It is a great idea to carry your notebook throughout instruction or have it in a reachable place. It is used to not only keep track of the lesson, but also to document behavior. During class time you may have to redirect behavior with students. When this happens, you want to take note of what the student was doing. Even if you create quick symbols and abbreviations to note the behavior, and later document completely, it is vital that it is recorded.

During parent/teacher conferences, the notebook will allow you to review dates and times to present it to an administrator or parent. This lets the parent and student know you are documenting the child, as well as interventions, to prevent disruptive behavior. Anytime you document a negative behavior, be prepared to intervene to prevent any reoccurrences by conferencing with the student or contacting the proper person. You want to show that not only was the behavior corrected on your behalf, but it was also followed up with an intervention.

I would create a table with four columns (see below) each school year that documented negative behavior. This sheet included each disruptive student. When it came time for a conference, I just highlighted the student's name and read it off to the parent in front of the student. By doing this, the student is now aware that you are keeping track of his or her behavior, and is less likely to continue any disruptions.

Referring back to dates and times is always difficult to argue against.

Student Intervention Log

Name	Date	Problem	Intervention (What did I do to solve the problem?)

The Facilitator

A lot of times as a teacher, one may become caught up in "teacher mode," where every aspect of the classroom is guided, directed, and practiced by the teacher. Let's stray away from this idea and put the responsibility on the student. Show your students what you want to be completed, and let them complete the task. It is easy to do the work for the child, how we want it completed, but sometimes teachers have to step back and allow growing in learning to occur. Students have become comfortable with the idea of the teacher doing all the work, but it is time to reverse that theory and put the bulk of the work on the student. As mentioned previously, students should feel "worked" when they exit your class. Allow students to take ownership in their education and be leaders amongst their peers. Practicing these qualities at an early age will make it easier as they continue on with their education and careers.

We, as educators, have to stray away from telling our students what to do in a step-by-step fashion, and let them discover their own learning through contemplation, inquiry, and experimenting. As a facilitator, you are walking around the classroom not only to maintain order, but also to observe student progress. Once you have lifted your class to the upper level of responsibility, you will be able to act as a facilitator and your job will become easier. You want your students to be able to stay on task even if you had to step into the hall momentarily or were away for a day.

When you have become a facilitator with minimum distractions, you have now conquered the obstacle of trying to run a smooth class. Although you may not notice that you have exerted classroom management, you will realize it when students are able to redirect disruptive behavior with their peers.

The *Trouble*some Student

There comes a time in everyone's teaching career when there is that one student who is committed to distracting other students. It is imperative after the second offense that contact is made with an administrator and parent to correct the negative behavior. You do not want to give any breathing room to a student who feels they can throw you, and the entire class, off task. The other students need to witness an intervention immediately, because they will have the tendency to mimic undesirable behavior if they see there are no consequences.

The majority of the time when a student is "acting out" it is because they are lacking in an area. For instance, they may not be able to read well or their comprehension is low. When this is the case, a child will disrupt the learning environment to keep anyone from noticing his or her learning disability.

When there is a student who is disruptive or combative, it is important not to engage in an argument with the student. Arguing, or going back and forth with a student, is what the child wants in order to lessen the instruction time. Cut off the conversation immediately and move on without giving attention to the student. If the student continues with disruption, ask him/her (politely) to step into the hall. Allow the student to wait on you for about five minutes (this builds anxiety in the student that can make him or her regain focus). When you speak with the student outside the classroom, do not tell him/her the reason they were sent out, but instead ask the student why he or she was asked to leave. By doing this you are making the student take ownership of his/her actions. Your role at this point is to act as an inquisitor by asking such questions as: Will this behavior continue? What is the importance of not being a distraction? Can I count on you to be focused? Are you a person of your word?

Allow the student to face their negative behavior, and at the same time take responsibility. This will also be the perfect time to reiterate consequences of negative behavior.

Remember, you are always the adult and can rectify the situation by simply saying, "Enough, Let's get focused." Don't forget to document the behavior and intervention.

Remain Calm

We do not live in a perfect world, so you will not have perfect students. When you become overwhelmed with the daily task of teaching and monitoring student behavior, you have to remember to remain calm at all times. As mentioned previously, when you encounter the troublesome student, you cannot show your frustration. The calmer you are, the easier it is to diffuse the situation.

Sometimes students will behave in a way to provoke the teacher, but do not let the student gain control over your feelings and cause you to erupt. It is safe to practice deep breaths throughout the school day to release those calming hormones called endorphins. The calmer you are as a teacher, the calmer your students will be. Raising your voice is something you should refrain from doing, because you do not want to stress yourself out; the louder you become will have an equal effect on your students. You do not want to promote a chaotic environment.

Another strategy to remain calm is simply folding your hands (not crossing your arms) across your mid-section and then talking to the disruptive student. For some reason, this assists with remaining calm in an uproarious atmosphere.

Remember, your students are watching you and are very observant, even when you are not aware.

What strategy will you use to remain calm?

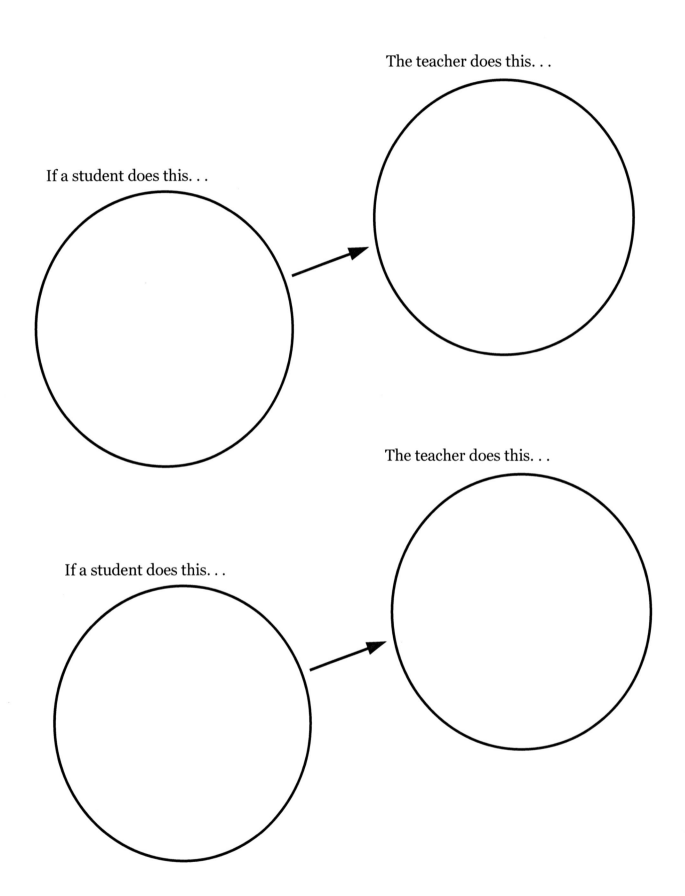

The teacher does this. . .

If a student does this. . .

The teacher does this. . .

If a student does this. . .

NOTES

When the Teacher is Away

Think back to when you were in school and your teacher was out. You may have breathed a sigh of relief thinking you were going to have a day of no work. You never want your students to expect to have a free day when you are away. It is an excellent idea to create a lesson plan that is used for substitute teachers only.

These lessons will consist of activities that are easy for the substitute to present and easy for the students to complete. When preparing a lesson for a substitute, keep in mind that he or she is not there to teach your class, but to merely "supervise." The substitute may not be familiar with your content, so you should not trust the idea of him/her teaching a lesson to your students.

Always remind your students throughout the course of the marking period that anytime you are away they are expected to be on their best behavior. It is important to leave a behavior log and seating chart for the substitute. Inform the teacher to let the students know that anyone who is not in their assigned seat will be marked absent. This is another good reason to have assigned seating in the class. By doing this, you are able to get feedback from the teacher on any student who displays disruptive behavior. If you receive a negative report from the substitute, make sure you inform the students of the report and implement consequences for their actions. When giving consequences, make sure it is memorable enough that the students will not want to receive another negative report. Incentives should also be given for good reports.

Let your students know they are accountable for one another when you are away. Sometimes students will blame one or two students for the distractions, and feel mistreated if they are punished for someone else's behavior. That is why you instill the responsibility onto the students and constantly remind them "WE are a class (unity)." This unity will also create strong relationships among the students, and will eliminate bullying and 'enemy' relationships between students.

Teacher's Name_____

Teacher's Email_____

Class Behavior Chart	
Class Period	**Behavior**

Students should be aware the substitute teacher is documenting their behavior so that they are motivated to display positive behavior. It is a good idea to ask for the teacher's contact information for future purposes. If possible, once you have the perfect candidate to maintain your classes while you are away, try to request the same person. You want your students to have a sense of respect and consistency for the person who is taking over your class temporarily.

When a Student is Away

Students will be absent throughout the course of the school year, and it can become frustrating when a student comes to you in the beginning of class asking for their missed assignments. To eliminate confusion, there should be a designated area in the classroom where students can go to retrieve any missed assignments. This area should be labeled and updated each day.

This area should include a large binder and five baskets. The binder is used to keep track of the agenda and notes. A responsible student can be assigned to fill out the binder each day, copying the agenda, taking any notes that may have been presented, and documenting the homework assignment. The five baskets are for each day of the week. Therefore, if a student misses more than one day they can pick up the appropriate assignment for that day.

Students should be aware that they are responsible for retrieving their assignments, because you have done your part by making it available. This will eliminate any questions on what the student missed while they were out, and it is an easy way to gather assignments if a parent wants to pick up their child's work. It is up to you how long you would like to keep the information available. Students should know the appropriate time to check the binder. You do not want a student getting up in the middle of instruction to retrieve assignments. You may want to inform students to check the assignments before or after class. Make sure students are aware that they are responsible for their missed work. The procedure for retrieving missed assignments should be included in the course syllabus so parents are informed as well. It may also be a good idea to give the students a time limit. For instance, if they missed one day than they have one day to get the assignment completed and turned in.

In my class I had a section labeled "Homework Center" that included a large calendar where I could indicate the homework assignment, baskets on the table, and a binder with the daily agenda. Students knew where to get any missed work and it eliminated any confusion or explanation on my part of what the student missed. The binder also helped if there was a new student and they needed notes. They were able to go to the binder and copy notes without relying on a fellow student. This also helps with parent conferences. If a parent wants to know the daily tasks and what their son or daughter has been learning, it is readily available for them. All in all, the homework center is beneficial in various aspects.

How will you keep your students informed in regards to daily activities?

Name_____

Objective_____

What will your binder include?

-
-
-
-
-
-
-
-
-

NOTES

What will be your process of students retrieving assignments?

_____

_____

_____

_____

_____

_____

_____

_____

_____

_____

_____

_____

_____

_____

_____

_____

_____

_____

_____

_____

_____

_____

_____

_____

_____

_____

Incentives

Incentives are used as a positive reinforcement to get your desired behavior from students. For instance, allowing students to earn homework passes for continuously completing assignments will encourage other students to want to complete their assignments. Giving treats or points for participation is also helpful to increase desired behavior. Most importantly, students love to be praised when they are on the right track. We must never forget to praise students when they are displaying positive behavior, especially to those who are improving.

Rewarding students for good behavior when there is a substitute is another way for students to be on their best behavior when you are away.

Desired Behavior

Reward

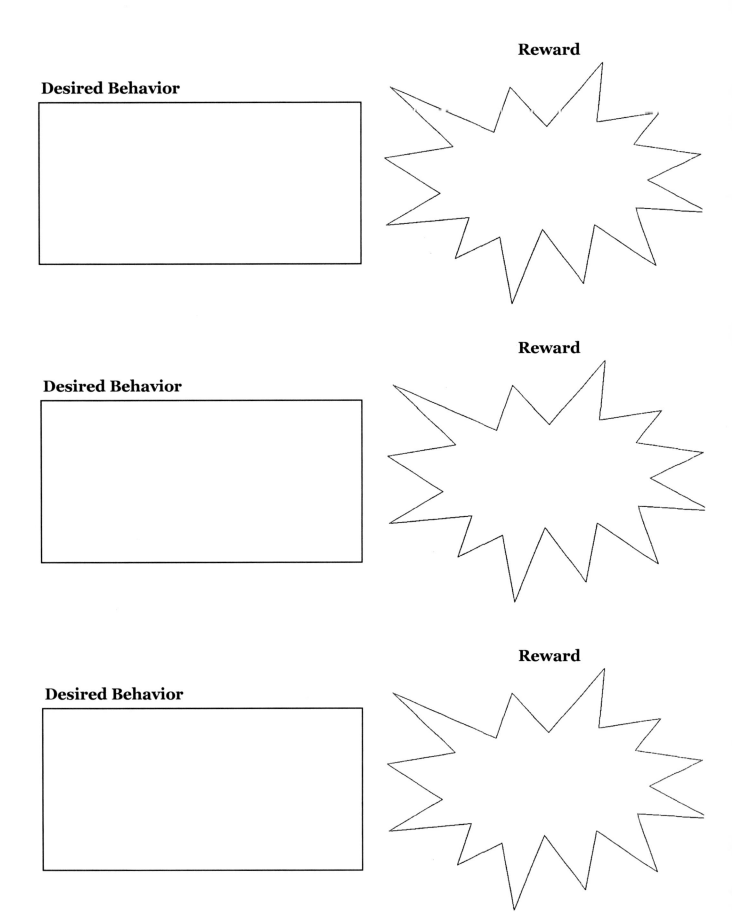

Desired Behavior

Reward

Desired Behavior

Reward

A Little Advice

• Always be aware of your word choice and the way you approach students. Students respond better to a negative situation when a teacher's approach is positive.

• Never tell your students that you are giving them a grade, but rather that they are *earning* a grade. You do not want the students to ever feel their grades are based on personal feelings, but instead the effort they put forth.

• Always be able to pull and show students how they earned their grade, and let them know they are the ones who complete the work. You are just a recorder placing the grade in the computer. Students must know at all times their grades depend on their efforts.

• Remember to keep accurate documentation.

• Always challenge yourself. Whether it's with a student or concept, you want to keep your job interesting.

• Try new techniques and ways of teaching. As a teacher we should always have room to grow and learn.

• Avoid confrontations with students. Have multiple ways of diffusing tensions quickly.

• Keep the parents informed about what is going on in the classroom and their child; you never want a parent to say, "I didn't know."

• As teachers, we need to be three steps ahead of the student, and be prepared for "worst case scenarios." Three steps means always having three answers and solutions; we do not want to only be one step ahead, because that step may fail.

• It may be helpful to post student grades in the classroom, indicating assignments and grade by student number to maintain confidentiality.

NOTES

Successful Days

Once you have practiced the techniques of this handbook, you may now expect successful days to come. Continued practice will make your teaching experience rewarding, and students will respect the effort that you are applying to ensure their success.

Sometimes students are unable to grasp the concept of a lesson because of disruptions around them, and managing a class well ceases disruption to the learning atmosphere. Practicing this management will allow the teacher to cater to the needs of students who are considered "at risk," and who suffer from learning disabilities. You want your classroom to be organized and respectful, so every student has the opportunity to learn.

Practicing disciplined classroom management will also allow teachers to have positive observation feedback and increased test scores, because students are learning the concept taught.

Of course some students enjoy being in class when the teacher is not implementing classroom management skills. They feel they are getting a "free day." However, once this idea is diminished they will actually seek to learn. Students should be trained on what behavior to display in the classroom, and it is the teacher's job to inform the student of proper behavior.

Teaching goes beyond the classroom. We are the most influential people in a student's educational life. If teachers everywhere practiced strong classroom management skills, it would positively impact the lives of students. Hopefully, this behavior can be displayed in other aspects of students' lives. Students should know the importance of education and why it is important not to disrupt the learning atmosphere.

After proper implementation of classroom management, the teacher can take learning to various levels by venturing to new and interesting places on field trips. It first starts in the classroom, but eventually evolves as everything else will fall into place. Instead of students not liking school, they will begin to enjoy coming to school because they are not worried about being bored, not learning, or feeling "out of place." This is the start of many successful days! There are many hidden talents in students that are just begging to be revealed, and you now have the key to unlocking them!

Teacher Reflection

Rate your day on a scale from 1-5, with 5 being a successful day.

******Day 1 Rate: 1   2   3   4   5   (circle one)******

Why did you choose this rate?_____

_____

_____

_____

_____

How will you improve for the next day?_____

_____

_____

_____

_____

******Day 1 Lesson Rate: 1   2   3   4   5   (circle one)******

Why did you choose this rate?_____

_____

_____

_____

_____

_____

How will you improve the lesson?_____

_____

_____

_____

_____

Teacher Reflection (classroom management)

Rate your classroom management on a scale from 1-5, with 5 being a successful day.

******Student behavior: 1   2   3   4   5   (circle one)******

Successful area of management: _____

_____

_____

_____

Area of improvement:_____

_____

_____

_____

How will you go about improving targeted area?_____

_____

_____

_____

******Classroom Structure: 1   2   3   4   5   (circle one)******

How did the structure facilitate managing? _____

_____

_____

_____

_____

Should the classroom be restructured for successful managing, if so how?_____

_____

_____

_____

_____

Reflect

Reflect

Teacher Reflection

Rate your day on a scale from 1-5, with 5 being a successful day.

******Day 2 Rate: 1   2   3   4   5   (circle one)******

Why did you choose this rate?_____

_____

_____

_____

_____

How will you improve for the next day?_____

_____

_____

_____

_____

******Day 2 Lesson Rate: 1   2   3   4   5   (circle one)******

Why did you choose this rate?_____

_____

_____

_____

_____

How will you improve the lesson?_____

_____

_____

_____

_____

Teacher Reflection (classroom management)

Rate your classroom management on a scale from 1-5, with 5 being a successful day.

******Student behavior: 1   2   3   4   5   (circle one)******

Successful area of management: _____
_____
_____
_____

Area of improvement:_____
_____
_____
_____

How will you go about improving targeted area?_____
_____
_____
_____

******Classroom Structure: 1   2   3   4   5   (circle one)******

How did the structure facilitate managing? _____
_____
_____
_____
_____

Should the classroom be restructured for successful managing, if so how?_____
_____
_____
_____
_____

Reflect

Reflect

Teacher Reflection

Rate your day on a scale from 1-5, with 5 being a successful day.

******Day 3 Rate: 1   2   3   4   5   (circle one)******

Why did you choose this rate?_____

_____

_____

_____

_____

_____

How will you improve for the next day?_____

_____

_____

_____

_____

_____

******Day 3 Lesson Rate: 1   2   3   4   5   (circle one)******

Why did you choose this rate?_____

_____

_____

_____

_____

_____

How will you improve the lesson?_____

_____

_____

_____

_____

Teacher Reflection (classroom management)

Rate your classroom management on a scale from 1-5, with 5 being a successful day.

******Student behavior: 1   2   3   4   5 (circle one)******

Successful area of management: _____
_____
_____
_____

Area of improvement: _____
_____
_____
_____

How will you go about improving targeted area? _____
_____
_____
_____

******Classroom Structure: 1   2   3   4   5 (circle one)******

How did the structure facilitate managing? _____
_____
_____
_____
_____

Should the classroom be restructured for successful managing, if so how? _____
_____
_____
_____

Reflect

Reflect

Teacher Reflection

Rate your day on a scale from 1-5, with 5 being a successful day.

******Day 4 Rate: 1   2   3   4   5   (circle one)******

Why did you choose this rate?_____

_____

_____

_____

_____

_____

How will you improve for the next day?_____

_____

_____

_____

_____

******Day 4 Lesson Rate: 1   2   3   4   5   (circle one)******

Why did you choose this rate?_____

_____

_____

_____

_____

_____

How will you improve the lesson?_____

_____

_____

_____

_____

Teacher Reflection (classroom management)

Rate your classroom management on a scale from 1-5, with 5 being a successful day.

******Student behavior: 1   2   3   4   5   (circle one)******

Successful area of management: _____
_____
_____
_____

Area of improvement:_____
_____
_____
_____

How will you go about improving targeted area?_____
_____
_____
_____

******Classroom Structure: 1   2   3   4   5   (circle one)******

How did the structure facilitate managing? _____
_____
_____
_____
_____

Should the classroom be restructured for successful managing, if so how?_____
_____
_____
_____
_____

Reflect

Reflect

Teacher Reflection

Rate your day on a scale from 1-5, with 5 being a successful day.

******Day 5 Rate: 1   2   3   4   5   (circle one)******

Why did you choose this rate?_____

_____

_____

_____

_____

_____

How will you improve for the next day?_____

_____

_____

_____

_____

******Day 5 Lesson Rate: 1   2   3   4   5   (circle one)******

Why did you choose this rate?_____

_____

_____

_____

_____

_____

How will you improve the lesson?_____

_____

_____

_____

_____

Teacher Reflection (classroom management)

Rate your classroom management on a scale from 1-5, with 5 being a successful day.

******Student behavior: 1   2   3   4   5   (circle one)******

Successful area of management: _____

_____

_____

_____

Area of improvement:_____

_____

_____

_____

How will you go about improving targeted area?_____

_____

_____

_____

******Classroom Structure: 1   2   3   4   5   (circle one)******

How did the structure facilitate managing? _____

_____

_____

_____

_____

Should the classroom be restructured for successful managing, if so how?_____

_____

_____

_____

Reflect

Reflect

Thank you for allowing me to share some of my methods and strategies with you that have been successful in my teaching career. I hope you have been inspired in some way to take control of your classrooms. I appreciate your support! Teachers rock!!!!

Teresa Mitchell has always had a passion for learning and teaching. As a child she enjoyed playing school and teaching younger members of her family. Although she veered away from education in the beginning of her college career, she was soon magnetized back to what she loved-- teaching. Being in the classroom 7+ years she has always been acknowledged for maintaining a well-managed classroom. She believes in order to teach, you have to have control, and in order to have control it has to be taught.

As an educator Teresa enjoyed the challenges that have arisen in today's educational system, due to the idea of creating a new way to overcome the hurdles. Her desire to teach and create global citizens amongst her students has driven her to create an instructional tool for teachers to help ease problems in their classrooms. She believes that she is limited in her classroom because she is only able to reach her students, but with this book she is able to reach multiple students when the methods are practiced across the nation.

In the future Teresa looks forward to creating programs for students and teachers to help close the academic gap and change the realm and outlook on education. She believes each student should receive the same education no matter their background or socioeconomic status.

Through hard work and dedication Teresa will continue to strive and search for ways to create a learning environment conducive to learning for the well-being of the educational system.

CPSIA information can be obtained at www.ICGtesting.com
Printed in the USA
BVOW03s1541210815

414021BV00009B/72/P

9 781937 165871